The Only Apple iPhone 6 Guide That You Will Ever Need

AMARPREET SINGH

Publisher - The Thought Flame

info@thethoughtflame.com

www.thethoughtflame.com

Table of Contents

Introduction

This book contains proven steps and strategies on how to use the iPhone 6 to unlock its full potential.

In this eBook you will find a step-by-step guide on how to use the iPhone 6 and how to utilize all of the features that are exclusive with this phone. On top of that you will learn some helpful tips and tricks to navigating the new iOS 8.

Whether you already own an iPhone 6 or whether you are thinking about getting one, this eBook will help you to understand the new iOS 8 system as well as learning basic functions of the phone such as turning the phone on and off.

Thanks again for downloading this book, I hope you enjoy it!

Chapter One: All About Your iPhone 6

If you want to maximize the capabilities of your powerful new smartphone, then you need to know its parts and specs first. One of the biggest reasons why Apple's new device is a big hit is that it is packed with a lot of cool features. The camera can now capture crisper and clearer images, and it has new processors that can handle intense graphics and complicated tasks.

The company also changed the appearance of the iPhone. With the popularity of larger screens, Apple jumped in on the bandwagon and developed a mobile device that is Herculean in size. While most critics jeered at the company for conforming to the standards of other brands, a lot of loyal fans still believed that this is a great innovation for the smartphone.

The Display of Your iPhone 6

Both iPhone 6 and iPhone 6 Plus have similar designs, but the biggest difference is their size. Of course, the one with the "Plus" on its name is the larger of the two.

The iPhone 6 Plus has a 5.5 inch display, making it perfect for people who have bigger hands. Its other iteration, meanwhile, has a 4.7 screen.

Since both devices now have larger displays, it means that they have better display resolution rates. The 6 Plus boasts an impressive 1920 X 1,080 in-plane switching screen with 401 ppi. This means that you can watch high definition videos clearly. The iPhone 6, on the other hand, has a 1,344 x 750 IPS display with 326 ppi. It is a little bit low compared to its bigger counterpart, but you do not have to worry about anything because it still produces crisper visuals compared to other smartphone models.

The Design of Your iPhone 6

Both smartphones from Apple have a curved metal frame that is similar to the HTC One M8. However, it still has unique qualities that make it an Apple device. The company is really obsessed with making smartphones that are compact and easy to bring anywhere, which is totally not a bad thing. Even though iPhone 6 and the 6 Plus have bigger displays, they are still thinner than their old predecessors. Their matte aluminum body feels good in the hands, and they don't have those chamfered edges that were found on the iPhone 5 before. The front is covered by durable glass, giving it a sleek and shiny look.

The round edges and glass front is a very common and highly popular look among other smartphone brands, so if it's your first time to use an Apple device, you will not feel too alienated.

Apple also changed the position of their buttons so that it can match the design of its competitors. Now, the power and lock button are placed on the right side. Even though the iPhone lost its distinct design, this change is needed, considering that the new device has a bigger build. However, the volume buttons can still be found on the left side. The only difference is that it has a wider and flatter appearance. Both devices sport a 3.5-millimeter headphone jack placed at the bottom of the device, right next to the holes that act as a speaker.

Just like any other Apple mobile device, the two new smartphones have a home button underneath the screen. It is still found on the front and center. Both smartphones are also equipped with Touch ID sensors. For those who have not yet used an iPhone 5S before, the Touch ID sensor is an innovative security technology that uses your thumb's fingerprint as the password, but what if the thief decides to cut your thumb? Relax, because this nifty security measure can identify a live and dead finger. Amongst all the other fingerprint scanners out there, the Touch ID sensor is the most reliable.

The Processor and Memory of The iPhone 6

If you thought that the A7 chip from the previous iPhone 5S will not get any better, wait till you see the new iPhone's Apple A8 processor. Just like the former chip, this one can handle more complex processes and detailed graphics. This means that you can edit media, watch videos, play 3D games, or take pictures without experiencing any lags or delays. These Apple A8 processors are clocked at 1.38 GHz, so you can browse the internet at lightning-fast speeds.

In addition, to powerful CPU, it is also equipped with a decent 1 GB of random-access memory (RAM). It may not be as big as other smartphone models, but this RAM is enough to let you multi-task in peace.

Unfortunately, the newer iPhone models still do not have any external memory card slot. However, the good news is that they now have bigger internal memory. Before, these mobile devices only have 16 GB to 64 GB capacity, but now, their internal memory can reach up to 128 GB. Of course, you have to pay a little extra for that.

The Operating System of The iPhone 6

Both mobile devices run on the latest iOS 8 operating systems. This new OS boasts of nifty security features, as well as a sleeker user interface. In addition, it also boasts of easier navigation.

The Camera of The iPhone 6

Another good thing about the new iPhone 6 and 6 Plus is that their front and rear snappers are upgraded. Both smartphones boast of an 8-megapixel rear camera, however, the bigger model has nifty optical image stabilization capabilities. This means that you can take sharper images even though your subject is moving.

Both devices also have a video stabilization feature, providing smoother and clearer video clips. You can now record 1080p videos and can capture 60 frames per second.

Their front-facing camera, on the other hand, is not blessed with an image stabilization feature. However, it does have an improved aperture.

With an f/ 2.2 aperture, it can absorb more light, thus making your selfies look much better.

The Battery Life

Both devices have improved battery lives. However, since the 6 Plus is bigger, expect that it can last longer. This big smartphone has a 13-hour battery life, while the smaller one can last for 10 hours. Results might vary depending on how you use your mobile device.

Chapter Two: Understanding The iOS 8 System

Aside from developing new iPhone devices, Apple also launched a new operating system called iOS 8 two days before releasing the iPhone 6 and 6 Plus. This new system packs a lot of new features that greatly compliment their new devices, and improve some of the capabilities of Apple's older phones.

One of the core features here is the ability to pay goods and services via Apple pay – a new system that uses near frequency chips (NFC) for payment instead of real money. In addition, the company is also letting third-party software developers to access some of their main features such as the keyboard and camera.

iOS 8 also enhanced the features that you have already loved in the iOS 7. It may not have such massive changes in terms of appearance, but it is really something that you should download if you want to have a fun and easy mobile experience when using your Apple device.

Messaging Feature

A great feature that you should look out for in the new iOS 8 is the improvement in the Messages app. Apple understands that third-party messaging apps such as Kik or Whatsapp have become very popular these days. That is why they wanted to make your online messaging experience better.

First, you can now find a details page on the upper right portion of the text message. On this page, you can see his contact information and there are also options to call that person or initiate a Facetime chat. Underneath the text, you can transfer a map of your current location to your contacts - a feature that is very similar to the Whatsapp Messenger.

In addition, the company also included a new method in their messaging app that lets users record their voice. There is a microphone button on the right side of the screen; just hold it down and the audio will be instantly recorded. Afterwards, you can send it with a swiping motion. It is a simple yet perfect feature if you want to share music at a concert.

Improvements To The Keyboard

Don't you just hate it when your iPhone autocorrects your words even before you finish typing them? Say goodbye to these frustrating moments as Apple made great improvements to their virtual QWERTY keyboard so that it can easily adapt to your preferences and lingo.

With the Quick Type feature, you can have several word suggestions that are arranged on a panel on top of your keyboard. This feature is available in 16 different languages. As you further communicate with your friends and family, it will learn to adapt and predict some of the common words or phrases that you normally use.

Upgrades To Your Photo Library and Camera

Pictures are always an important thing for iPhone users. Thankfully, the iOS 8 packs a lot of cool features that will make the mobile shutterbugs and newbie photographers happy. First, the improved Photos app has auto-straightening, as well as cropping features. The app also has some built-in color correcting tools so that your images will look greater than before.

The camera app, on the other hand, allows users to create time-lapse videos. Similar to the other options such as the slow-mo, panorama and square, this new feature is also intuitive. Simply point your snapper at some busy intersection, moving flowers , or a herd of animals walking and start the recording process. Once you are finished, your device will generate a decent time-lapse clip that you can share with your friends via social media.

The camera app also has two new nifty sliders that let you adjust the exposure and color levels. Your device can now analyze the image so that it can make the right adjustments.

Siri Improvements

For faster results, your favorite virtual assistant can now stream any voice recognition. Siri supports 22 languages. In addition, you can now control Siri in a hands -free way. However, you need to plug in your iPhone to activate it. Therefore, whether you are charging on a study desk or inside vehicle, you can now activate this virtual assistant and ask her a question.

Apple Pay

Now, you can use your iPhone to buy goods and services in various popular stores . However, this only works for the new iPhone 6 and 6 Plus because they are the very first NFC enabled devices of Apple. You can use the camera on your phone to scan credit or bank cards.

Chapter Three: Button Layout

The iPhone 6 has a total of 5 buttons and one switch on the actual device. To control the phone it uses touchscreen capability. Each button on the phone has a variety of different functions, depending on how you use it in context.

The Home Button

This button is used to take you to the home screen of the iPhone 6. It also allows you to open many applications at once when it is pressed twice in a quick manner. When you hold the button it can be used to turn off the phone and to delete applications that you do not want.

The Volume Controls

This button controls the volume of the ringer. It also controls the volume of your earpiece or speakerphone when you are in mid conversation. It can also control the overall volume of media that is played on the phone.

The Vibration Switch

This button is used primarily to turn the vibration on or off the phone of to turn the sound completely off.

The Headphone Jack

This jack allows either headphone or speakers to be plugged into the phone. You can use an AUX cable to hook the phone to your car to allow music to be played over the speakers.

Lightning Connector

This outlet allows the phone to be connected to either a computer or a phone charger.

The Wake or Sleep Button

Located on the side of the phone this button allows you to turn the phone on or off and to lock or unlock the phone.

How To Charge The Phone

To ensure that the phone works well, please follow these guidelines:

Discharge the phone completely at least once a month for optimal performance. When charging the battery, the meter in the upper right-hand corner of the screen (when unlocked) may show that it is fully charged;

however, the charge is not complete until 100% Charged appears on the lock screen. Insert the Lightning cable into the Lightning Connector on the bottom of the phone.

Once the lightning cable is inserted correctly, an indicator sound will sound over the phone or the phone itself will vibrate.

How to Turn Your Phone Off and One

Turning The Phone On: Use the Sleep/Wake button to turn the phone on or off. To turn the phone on, press and hold the Sleep/Wake button for two seconds. Once the phone turns on the apple logo will be displayed. After the phone has finished starting up, the Lock screen is displayed.

Please note that if the phone does not turn on after a few seconds, try charging the battery.

Turning The Phone Off: To turn the phone off, press and hold the Sleep/Wake button until the screen becomes dark. The message "Slide to power off" appears. Touch the slider and move your finger to the right. The phone turns off.

Please note that to keep the phone on, touch Cancel or do not take any action at all.

How To Install A Sim Card

Insert the SIM card from an old phone to retain your personal information and phone number. The type of SIM card depends on your carrier. For instance, you cannot insert a Verizon SIM card into an AT&T phone, and vice-versa.

To install a SIM card:

1. Insert the end of a paper clip or a SIM eject tool into the hole on the right side of the phone. The SIM card tray then will pop out.

2. Take out the old SIM card, if necessary, and insert the new SIM card with the short side facing upwards.

3. Re-insert the tray into the phone. You new SIM card is now installed.

Chapter Four: Hot To Set Up Your Phone

Step One

Turn on the phone by pressing and holding the Power button until the apple icon appears. The phone will start up and the Welcome screen will appear.

Step Two

Next, touch the screen anywhere and move your finger to the right to begin setting up your phone. The first thing you will need to do is set up the language settings. The Language screen will appear next. Touch a language in the list. The language is selected, and the Country screen will appear next. Touch the country where you reside.

Step Three

Once you select the country you live in, you will have to set up a Wi-Fi network. The country is selected, and the Wi-Fi Networks screen appears.

Step Four

Touch a Wi-Fi network and put in the appropriate password. Enter the network password, which can be found on your wireless router. Touch Join in the upper right-hand corner of the screen. The phone will then connect to the Wi-Fi network you have selected.

Step Five

Next you will have to activate your phone. If you did not activate your iPhone in the store, you may need to confirm your phone number before the Location Services screen appears. Enter your billing zip code and the last four digits of your social security number to confirm.

Step Six

Touch Enable Location Services if you want to turn the feature on. Touch Disable Location Services to leave the feature turned off. Some applications will not work with Location Services turned off.

Step Seven

The Set Up iPhone screen will appear next. Here you will need to touch Restore from iCloud Backup or Restore from iTunes Backup if you have a data backup. You will need to connect the phone to your computer and run iTunes if you touch 'Restore from iTunes Backup'. Touch Set Up as New iPhone if you do not have an iCloud or iTunes backup. The Apple ID screen appears.

Step Eight

Next touch Sign In with your Apple ID if you have an Apple ID or touch Create a Free Apple

ID. The Terms and Conditions screen appears once you are signed in. Touch Agree in the bottom right-hand corner of the screen. A confirmation dialog appears. Touch Agree again.

Step Nine

The iCloud screen will appear next. Touch Use iCloud to use the feature or touch Don't Use iCloud to disable it. The Find My iPhone feature is turned on automatically when you use iCloud.

Step Ten

The iMessage and FaceTime screen will appear next. Touch a phone number or email address if you would like to enable it for iMessage or FaceTime. A blue check mark appears next to each selected address or number. Touch Next in the upper right-hand corner of the screen when you are finished.

Step Eleven

The iCloud drive screen will appear next. iCloud Drive syncs all of your documents and images in iCloud, and updates them on all of your phone as you work. You will then need to touch Upgrade to iCloud Drive. The iCloud Drive will then be turned on, and the Passcode Creation screen appears.

Step Twelve

Enter a passcode to set up a security lock for your phone, or touch Don't Add Passcode to do it later. Next touch the iPhone on the left to view the most amount of information on your screen. However, the fonts will be slightly harder to read.

Step Thirteen

Next, touch the iPhone on the right to use your iPhone in zoomed view. Fonts will be easier to read, but the screen will not fit as much information. The Diagnostics screen appears.

Step Fourteen

Then Touch Automatically Send to have the phone send usage data to Apple or touch Don't Send to disable this feature. Usage Data contains anonymous statistics about the ways in which you use your phone.

Step Fifteen

Last touch Get Started and the phone setup will be complete.

Navigating The Screens of Your iPhone

There are many ways to navigate the phone. Use the following tips to quickly navigate the screens of the phone:

1. Use the Home button to return to the Home

screen at any time. Any application or tool that you were using will be in the same state when you return to it.

2. At the Home screen, slide your finger to the left to access additional pages. If nothing happens, the other pages are blank.

3. Touch the center of the Home screen and slide your finger down to access the phone's search feature. You may search any data stored on your phone, including application data, as well as the web, iTunes, Application Store, movie show times, locations nearby, and much more.

Organizing The Icons On Your Home Screen

You may wish to re-order the location of the application icons on the screens. To organize application icons:

1. Touch an icon and hold it until all of the icons begin to shake. The icons can now be moved around the screen.

2. Move the icon to the desired location and let go of the screen. The icon is relocated and the surrounding icons are re-ordered accordingly. If an icon that used to be on the screen is gone, then it has been moved to a different Home screen in the process.

3. To move an icon to another screen, move the icon to the edge of the current one and hold it there. The adjacent screen appears. Drop the icon in the desired location.

4. Press the Home button. The icons stop shaking.

Chapter Five: Making Both Video and Voice Calls With The iPhone 6

Numbers that are not in your Phonebook can be dialed on the keypad. To manually dial a phone number, touch the phone icon on the Home screen. The keypad will then appear. Touch the phone icon at the bottom of the screen, if you do not see the keypad. Enter the desired phone number and then touch the phone icon at the bottom of the screen. The phone dials the number.

Calling A Contact From Your Contact List

If a number is stored in your Phonebook, you may touch the name of a contact to dial it. To call a contact already stored in your phone:

1. Touch the icon on the Home screen. The Phonebook will then appear.

2.Touch the name of the desired contact. The Contact Information screen will then appear.

3.Touch the desired phone number. The phone calls the contact's number.

Calling A Friend On Your Favorite List

There is no Speed Dial feature on phone. Instead, frequently dialed numbers can be saved as Favorites, which can be accessed more quickly than other contacts. To call a number stored in Favorites:

1. Touch the phone icon on the Home screen. The keypad screen will then appear.

2. Touch the star icon at the bottom of the screen. The Favorites screen will then appear.

3. Touch the name of a Favorite. The device will then call the selected number.

How To Receive A Voice Call

There are several ways to accept or reject a voice call based on whether or not the screen is locked. Use the following tips when receiving a voice call:

1. To receive an incoming voice call while the phone is locked, touch and move the arrow icon on the slider. The call will then be answered.

2. To mute the ringer, press the Sleep/Wake button. To reject the incoming call, press the Sleep/Wake button again.

3. To receive an incoming call while using an application (or viewing a Home screen), touch

the phone button.

4. To reject the incoming call, touch the button. The call will then be declined. The number then appears in red in the list of recent calls, signifying that it is a missed call, and a notification appears above the red phone icon on the Home screen.

Reply To A Call With A Text Message

During an incoming call, you may reject it and automatically send a text message to the caller. To reply to an incoming call with a text message:

1. Touch Message during an incoming voice call. A list of pre-defined text messages appear.

2. Touch a message. The selected text message is sent to the caller. Alternatively, touch

Custom to enter your own text message.

3. Touch the send button. The phone sends the custom text message to the caller.

How To Use The Speakerphone During A Call

The phone has a built-in Speakerphone, which is useful when calling from a car or when several people need to hear the conversation. To use the Speakerphone during a phone call:

1. Place a voice call. The Calling Screen will then appear.

2. Touch the speaker icon. The Speakerphone is turned on. Adjust the volume of the Speakerphone by using the Volume Controls.

3. Touch the speaker icon. The Speakerphone is turned off.

Adding A Conference Call

To talk to more than one person at a time, call another person while continuing the current call. To create a conference call, place a voice call and then touch the plus icon. The list of contacts or the keypad is shown. Dial a number or select a contact to call. The first contact is put on hold while the phone dials and connects to the second. Touch the plus icon. A three-way conference call will then be created.

Starting A Facetime Call

You can place a video call to another iPhone, iPad, Mac, or iPod (third generation and higher). Facetime does not require a Wi-Fi connection. You can place and receive calls using a 4G connection (provided that you have at least one bar of service). However, using Wi-Fi may still provide a better video calling experience.

1. Touch the phone icon on the Home screen. The keypad appears.

2. Touch Contacts at the bottom of the screen. The Phonebook appears.

3. Touch the name of a contact. The Contact Information screen appears.

4. Touch the video camera icon to place a FaceTime call. A high-pitched beeping sound plays until the call connects.

5. Touch the camera with two arrows icon at any time to switch cameras. Using this feature, you can either show your contact what you are seeing or show them your face.

6. The iPhone 6 can also receive FaceTime calls. To receive an incoming FaceTime call, touch Accept.

Conclusion

Thank you again for downloading this book!

I hope this book was able to help you to learn how to use your Apple iPhone 6 while also enjoying the variety of features that this phone has to offer.

The next step is to begin using your Apple iPhone 6 to the best of your ability to have fun using all of the exclusive features that this phone has to offer.

About Us

The Thought Flame is committed to add value to its customers through various books, online courses and other resources. You can learn more about us and our books at www.thethoughtflame.com.

Don't forget to check out our amazing **online video courses** at www.thethoughtflame.com/courses/ to take your knowledge to another level.

To check out our **extraordinary collection of diet/cookbooks**, visit http://www.thethoughtflame.com/category/non-fictional/cookbooks/ .

As a part of our valued relationship with our customers, we keep providing you free promotional books, courses and other stuff on subscribing with us on our site. We have a strict anti-spam policy and assure you no spam mails will be sent to your mailbox.

To subscribe with us, visit www.thethoughtflame.com.

Like our work and would like to say thanks? Buy us a cup of coffee at www.thethoughtflame.com/coffee/

Author

Amarpreet Singh is an avid learner and his passion for education has made him travel, work and study all across the world. He holds three masters degrees, including MBA, from top universities in Asia.

He is author of dozens of books, many of which are Amazon's bestseller, varying in various topics and categories. He also teaches many online courses having thousands of students across the world.

He has a keen interest in international affairs, economics, global poverty and politics, financial markets and entrepreneurship, and strives to be part of a community that shares the same passion.

He has worked as consultant with organizations like Airbus and The World Bank. He loves travelling and learning about new cultures, and has been fortunate to live/work/travel/study in countries like India, China, Korea, US, South Africa, Japan, Philippines, Singapore, Canada etc., and learn about the culture and lifestyle in each of them. To check out more of his work, visit www.thethoughtflame.com